Chinese Heritage

Celebrating Diversity in My Classroom

By Tamra B. Orr

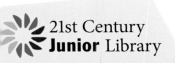
21st Century
Junior Library

CHERRY LAKE
Publishing

Published in the United States of America by
Cherry Lake Publishing
Ann Arbor, Michigan
www.cherrylakepublishing.com

Reading Adviser: Marla Conn MS, Ed., Literacy specialist, Read-Ability, Inc.

Photo Credits: © ESB Professional / Shutterstock Images, cover; © kikujungboy / Shutterstock Images, 4; © Chatchawat Prasertsom / Shutterstock Images, 6; © LP2 Studio / Shutterstock Images, 8; © DMHai / Shutterstock Images, 10; © LMspencer / Shutterstock Images, 12; © chartchy / Shutterstock Images, 14; © Maridav / Shutterstock Images, 16; © all_about_people / Shutterstock Images, 18; © Zhao jian kang / Shutterstock Images, 20

Library of Congress Cataloging-in-Publication Data
Name: Orr, Tamra, author.
Title: Chinese heritage / by Tamra B. Orr.
Description: Ann Arbor : Cherry Lake Publishing, 2018. | Series: Celebrating diversity in my classroom | Includes bibliographical references and index.
Identifiers: LCCN 2017033726 | ISBN 9781534107342 (hardcover) | ISBN 9781534109322 (pdf) | ISBN 9781534108332 (pbk.) | ISBN 9781534120310 (hosted ebook)
Subjects: LCSH: China—Juvenile literature.
Classification: LCC DS706 .O77 2018 | DDC 951—dc23
LC record available at https://lccn.loc.gov/2017033726

Cherry Lake Publishing would like to acknowledge the work of The Partnership for 21st Century Skills.
Please visit *www.p21.org* for more information.

Printed in the United States of America
Corporate Graphics

CONTENTS

The city of Guangzhou is China's third largest city.
More than 12 million people live there.

Charming China

China is part of East Asia. It is the fourth-largest country in the world. But China has the most people. An amazing 1.3 billion people live there. However, many people from China have also **emigrated** to other countries all over the world. There are about 2 million **immigrants** from China in the United States!

What is their home country like? Read along to find out!

Tai chi was developed for self defense,
but is now used to practice balance and relieve stress.

很高兴见到你

很高兴见到你! That means "Nice to meet you!" in Mandarin Chinese (pronounced hun gowsing jeean dow nee). Instead of using letters like many other languages, China uses symbols. While the English alphabet only has 26 letters, Chinese has more than 40,000 characters!

Did you know that you already know some Chinese words? Have you ever tried eating *tofu*? Do you know someone who has taken

Shih Tzu means "Lion Dog" in Mandarin Chinese.

lessons in *tai chi*? Have you ever seen a *Shih Tzu* puppy? All of those are Chinese words that are often heard in the United States.

How a person says words in Mandarin Chinese can change their meaning. This happens when the tone of voice is changed. Tone is the rising and falling of a person's voice while speaking. It gives words very different meanings.

Create!

Go online and find a website that shows you how to write your name in Chinese. Get paper and pen and see if you can copy the symbols. How hard—or fun—is it to make them?

The Chinese zodiac is based on the cycles of the moon.
There is one animal for each year in the lunar cycle.

Animals and a Giant

Are you a tiger? Could you be a dragon? Maybe you are a monkey or a snake? People from China believe the answer to this question depends on what year you were born. The Chinese **zodiac** is based on 12 different animals. Each animal has its own features. For example, if you were born in 2009, you would be an ox. According to the Chinese beliefs, this means you are

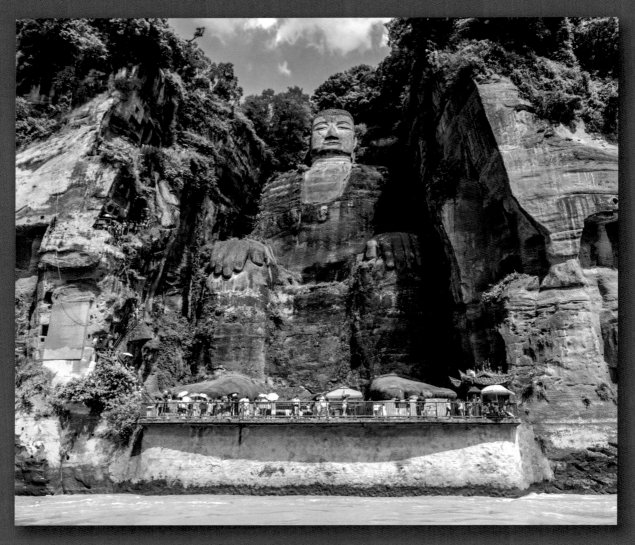

The Leshan Buddha's eyebrows are more than 18 feet (5.5 m) long!

strong, honest, and loyal. What if you were born in 2010? You would be a tiger. This means you are brave and charming.

The people of China celebrate many different religions. For thousands of years, some Chinese have followed **Buddhism**. This belief focuses on how to end pain and suffering in people's lives. In China's city of Leshan there is a huge statue of Buddha. It was carved out of stone more than 1,300 years ago. It took 90 years to complete. The statue is 233 feet (71 meters) high. Its shoulder is big enough to hold a basketball court.

Fried sesame balls are made of rice flour and filled with red bean paste.

Rice and Vinegar

Do you like rice? If you lived in China, you would think that is a very strange question. Of course you do! The Chinese eat more rice than any other people in the world. Rice is usually part of breakfast, lunch, and dinner. It is served with main dishes and as side dishes. It is an ingredient in everything from soups to desserts. But what goes with the rice changes from one part of China to another.

Tanghulu was originally a dessert made only in the winter.

Those from the west enjoy lamb with their rice. People from central China like spicy food with lots of garlic and ginger. In the east, they serve seafood since the ocean is close by. In the north, dishes with noodles and dumplings are popular. In the south, people like sour foods and use a lot of salt water and vinegar.

A favorite sweet treat is *tanghulu*. This Chinese candy is made from fruit dipped in liquid sugar and then dried. The fruits are usually crab apples, kiwi, or grapes.

Red symbolizes good luck. Red envelopes containing money
are given as gifts during the New Year.

A Brand-New Year

New Year's in the United States is often a fun holiday. Some cities light fireworks. People stay up until midnight to see one year end and another begin. The Chinese New Year (often called Spring Festival) is even bigger. It is held early in January or February and lasts for two weeks! In China, schools and businesses close for at least part of it.

Those two weeks are busy ones. Before the New Year starts, everyone cleans house. This sweeps out the bad luck and welcomes

Dragon boats usually carry 20 paddlers,
1 drummer to keep pace, and 1 steerer.

in good luck. Special food is cooked, including extra-long noodles. They are made to wish people long lives. Spring Festival has many parades. People wear costumes. Fireworks are lit to scare away any evil spirits.

There are other holidays, too. Women's Day is in March. The Dragon Boat Festival is usually in May. And National Day is in October. No matter what the Chinese are celebrating, they are sure to have fun!

Look!

Look at this photo of rowers during China's Dragon Boat Festival. Would it be fun to compete in this race? Why or why not? What muscles would you have to use to be a good rower?

GLOSSARY

Buddhism (BOO-diz-uhm) religion based on the teachings of a man named Buddha

emigrated (EM-ih-grayt-id) left your home country to live in another country

immigrants (IM-ih-gruhnts) people who have moved from one country to another and settled there

zodiac (ZOH-dee-ak) an imaginary band in the sky through which the sun, moon, and planets appear to move

Chinese Words

Shih Tzu (sheetz-zoo) a Chinese breed of dog known for its shiny fur

tai chi (tie-chee) a Chinese martial art and meditation exercise

tanghulu (tig-loo) candied fruit on a stick

tofu (tow-foo) cheese-like food made from soybeans

FIND OUT MORE

BOOKS

Branscombe, Allison. *All About China: Stories, Songs, Crafts and More for Kids.* North Clarendon, VT: Tuttle Publishing, 2014.

Murray, Julie. *China.* Minneapolis: ABDO Publishing, 2014.

Perkins, Chloe. *China.* New York: Simon Spotlight, 2016.

WEBSITES

National Geographic Kids—China

http://kids.nationalgeographic.com/explore/countries/china/#china-dragon.jpg
Facts about China's people, geography, language, and more at National Geographic Kids.

China Facts

www.kids-world-travel-guide.com/china-facts.html
Interesting China facts at Kids World Travel Guide.

Cool Kid Facts—China

www.coolkidfacts.com/china-facts-for-kids/
Facts about the people, economy, and government of China at Cool Kid Facts.

INDEX

ABOUT THE AUTHOR

Tamra Orr is the author of hundreds of books for readers of all ages. She graduated from Ball State University, but moved with her husband and four children to Oregon in 2001. She is a full-time author, and when she isn't researching and writing, she writes letters to friends all over the world. Orr enjoys life in the big city of Portland and feels very lucky to be surrounded by so much diversity.